W9-AXD-122

BUGS

BUGS:
Stingers Suckers Sweeties Swingers

LIZ GREENBACKER

FRANKLIN WATTS
NEW YORK / CHICAGO / LONDON / SYDNEY
A FIRST BOOK

Photographs copyright ©: Susan Van Etten, cover; Breck P. Kent, 2, 16, 19, 33 (top), 41; Vermont Travel Division, 6–7; John Mitchell/Photo Researchers, Inc., 9 (top); Hermann Eisenbeiss/Photo Researchers, Inc., 9 (bottom); Comstock, Inc., 10, 36, 44–45; Alpena Co./Photo Researchers, Inc., 12; Mella Panzella/Animals Animals, 13; Clemenz Photography, 14–15, 55; Visuals Unlimited, 18; Frederick D. Atwood, 20, 25; Carl W. Rettenmeyer, Connecticut Museum of Natural History, 21, 23, 51, 53; Frederick McDonald Photography, 26–27; Angelo Giampicciolo, 28; Dan Kline/Visuals Unlimited, 29; J. Alcock/Visuals Unlimited, 31; Harry Rogers/Photo Researchers, Inc., 32; James H. Robinson/Photo Researchers, Inc., 33 (bottom), 38, 47; Ron Singer, U.S. Fish & Wildlife Service, 35; C.W. Perkins/Animals Animals, 42; Scott Camazine/Photo Researchers, Inc., 46; Stephen Dalton/Photo Researchers, Inc., 48; Raymond Mendez/Animals Animals, 49.

Library of Congress Cataloging-in-Publication Data

Greenbacker, Liz.
Bugs : stingers, suckers, sweeties, swingers / Liz Greenbacker.
p. cm. — (A First book)
Includes bibliographical references and index.
Summary: Examines various insects and other crawling creatures found in and around the home, including grasshoppers, wasps, spiders, and ticks.
ISBN 0-531-20072-8 (HC, library binding)
1. Insects—Juvenile literature. [1. Insects.] I. Title. II. Series.
QL467.2.G75 1993
595.7—dc20
92-24963 CIP AC

Printed in the United States of America
6 5 4 3 2 1

CONTENTS

PART ONE: In the Woods

Chapter 1: Insects in a World of Their Own **6**

PART TWO: In the Fields

Chapter 2: Ticks, Grasshoppers, and Cicadas **14**

Chapter 3: The Stingers: Wasps and Hornets **21**

PART THREE: In the Garden

Chapter 4: The Suckers: Scales and Aphids **26**

Chapter 5: Lacewings and Ladybugs **33**

Chapter 6: The Sweeties: Bees **38**

PART FOUR: In the House

Chapter 7: Cockroaches, Flies, and Other House Dwellers **44**

Chapter 8: The Swingers: House Spiders **51**

GLOSSARY **56**

FOR FURTHER READING **60**

INDEX **61**

PART ONE: In the Woods

CHAPTER 1
Insects in a World of Their Own

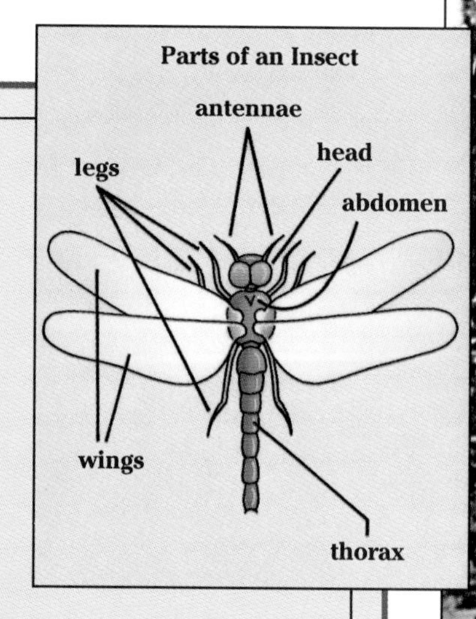

Common Name: Insect
Phylum: Arthropoda (joint-legged animals)
Class: Hexapoda (six-legged animals)
Number of species: 900,000
Habitat: All over the world
Life span: A range of one month to seventeen years
Diet: Trees, plants, animals, and other insects

Insects are fascinating creatures that affect our lives every day. Some have lived on Earth for 300 million years. Insects belong to the phylum, or category, called Arthropoda. All arthropods have jointed legs. Insects belong to the scientific class called Hexapoda because all insects have six jointed legs.

Insects have three body parts: head, *thorax*, and *abdomen*. All insects have a hard outer skin called the exoskeleton. Our skeleton is inside our body. Insects wear theirs on the outside. Insects also have *antennae* that are long, short, fat, thin, bent, or straight. Most insects have two pairs of wings. Insects grow differently from most other animals. Insects hatch from eggs and go through stages called *metamorphosis* to become adults.

Insects can help us and hurt us. To discover how important insects are, we'll look at all the places where they live. First we'll explore their natural surroundings, the places where humans visit but don't make changes.

When insects live in ponds, marshes, swamps, and woods, they help people. Insects are part of the *food chain* that makes carbon available so plants and trees can grow. *Carbon* is the *element* required for all life on Earth.

A pond is a good place to watch insects and to see a food chain in action. At first glance, a pond may appear peaceful and quiet, but for the creatures that live there it is a place of the hunter and the hunted. Animals hunt other animals. Frogs and birds hunt insects. Insects hunt other insects. Many animals eat the plants that grow around a pond. When all the dead plants, insects, and other animals decay, carbon is released to give life to more plants, more insects, and more animals.

Every pond is home for millions of insects. Let's meet a few of its residents.

Swimming underneath a pond's surface is a giant water bug that is 2 inches (5.08 cm) long. The giant water bug's forelegs look like a pair of curved tweezers lined with hooks. The bug uses its middle and hind legs to swim. Beware of giant water bugs. Their bite is as painful as a bee sting. This giant water bug can inflict a poisonous bite that can *paralyze* and suck out the body fluids of its prey. The giant water bug eats fish, tadpoles, snails, frogs, and small water snakes.

The easiest pond dweller to spot is the water strider. It is one of the fastest moving insects. There is an invisible, elastic film on top of all water called surface tension. Because the water strider's long, jointed feet have fine hairs that don't absorb water, this bug can "walk" on top of a pond without breaking through the water's surface. Water striders eat live or dead

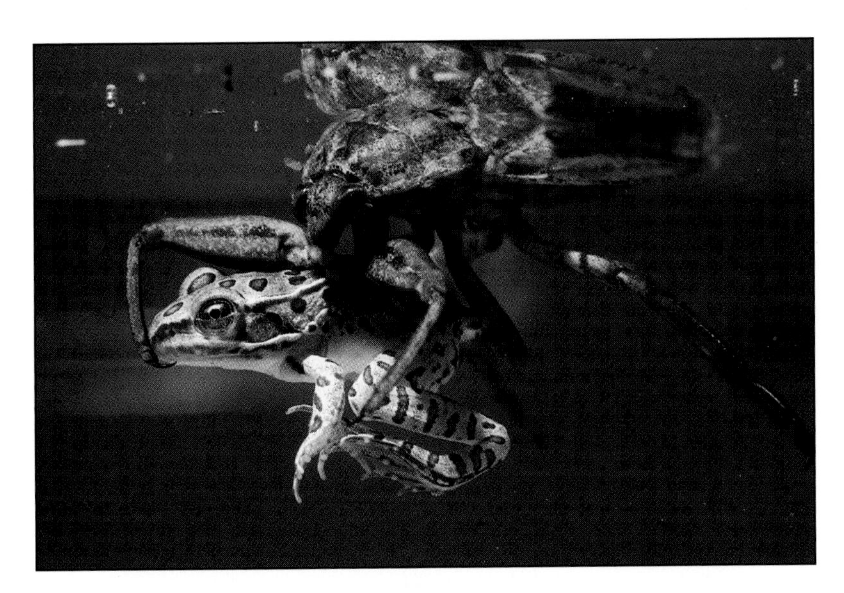

Top: A giant water bug captures and feeds on a frog.
Bottom: A water strider "walks" on the surface of a pond.

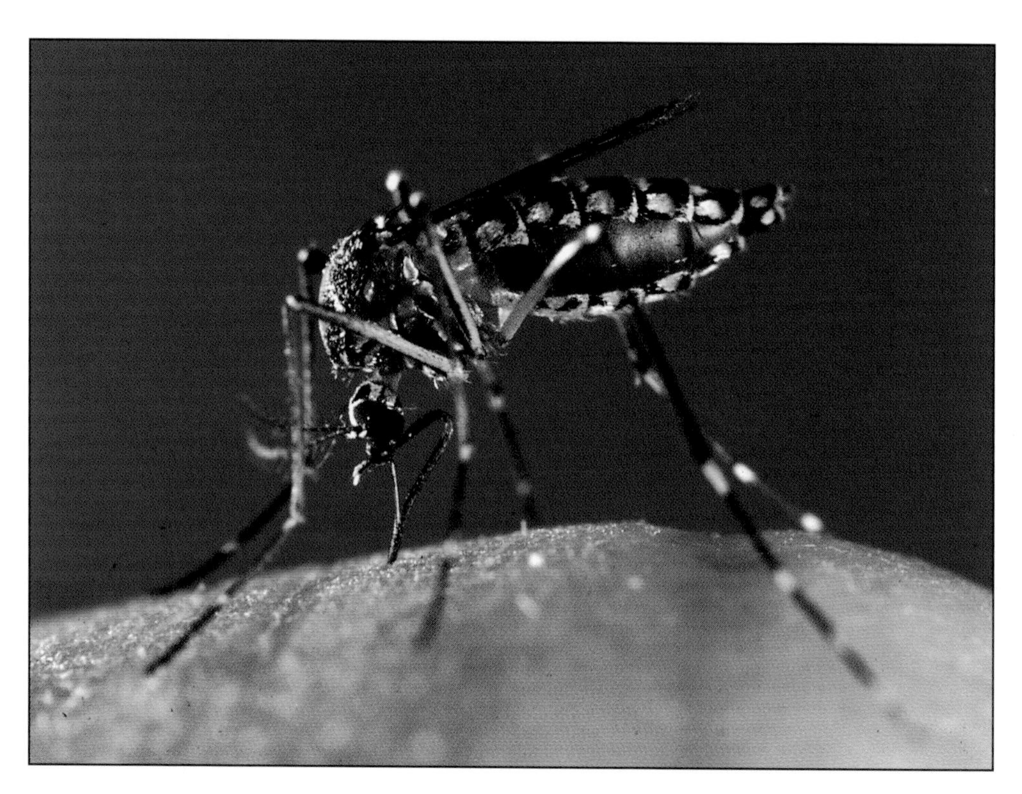

This adult female mosquito is feeding on a human.

insects or leftover insect parts dropped into a pond from the birds above.

Even people do not escape the food chain around a pond. As we enjoy the quiet, a female mosquito bites us on the leg. Full of our blood, she flies away to lay her *egg rafts*. She'll lay one hundred to four hundred eggs in a still patch of water.

There are more than three thousand different species of mosquitoes, and they live almost everywhere there is water, even on 14,000-foot (4,267 m) mountains and in 3,700-foot (1,128 m) deep gold mines. Mosquitoes can be dangerous because they can carry diseases, such as yellow fever. Victims of yellow fever suffer headaches, fever, and vomiting. Their nostrils, lips, and tongue turn red. After a few days, the patient's skin turns from red to lemon-yellow, which is how yellow fever got its name. Yellow fever from infected mosquito bites killed many soldiers during the Spanish-American War in 1898. During the Vietnam War, U.S. soldiers suffered from eleven different diseases spread by mosquitoes.

During the Spanish-American War, people controlled the threat posed by mosquitoes by emptying rain barrels, drying up mud puddles, and cleaning clogged drains. Cleaning and drying the places where mosquitoes laid their eggs stopped the mosquitoes from spreading the deadly diseases. It is easier to kill mosquitoes in their larval stage. A very thin film of oil poured on pond surfaces makes it impossible for the *larvae* to breathe.

The dragonfly, that large, colorful fast flier with lacy wings, is the mosquito's natural enemy. Thanks to dragonflies, birds, spiders, and frogs, the number of mosquitoes is controlled even around ponds.

The beautiful widow dragonfly helps keep the mosquito population low.

A food chain is a place of hunter and hunted. Here a barking tree frog eats a grasshopper.

Other residents of ponds are flies, bees, wasps, butterflies, moths, and even cockroaches. All play an important part in the food chain. Every creature around a pond lives and dies to promote life. No insect lives only to bother people. But wherever people alter the natural food chain to plant crops, build homes, or grow gardens, we dislocate or destroy the natural enemies of insects. Then insects can increase in number and do more harm than good. Even so, nature still provides us with ways to control them—through other insects!

PART TWO: In the Fields

CHAPTER 2
Ticks, Grasshoppers, and Cicadas

Common Name: Tick
Class: Arachnida
Order: Acarina
Number of species: 30,000
Habitat: Grass and moss of forests and fields
Life span: One month as adult
Diet: Blood of animals and humans

Ticks are *arachnids*, not insects, because they have eight legs while insects have six. An adult tick is as tiny as the head of a pin. A young tick, or *nymph*, is even smaller. Ticks live in woods, fields, and even in tall grasses around our back-

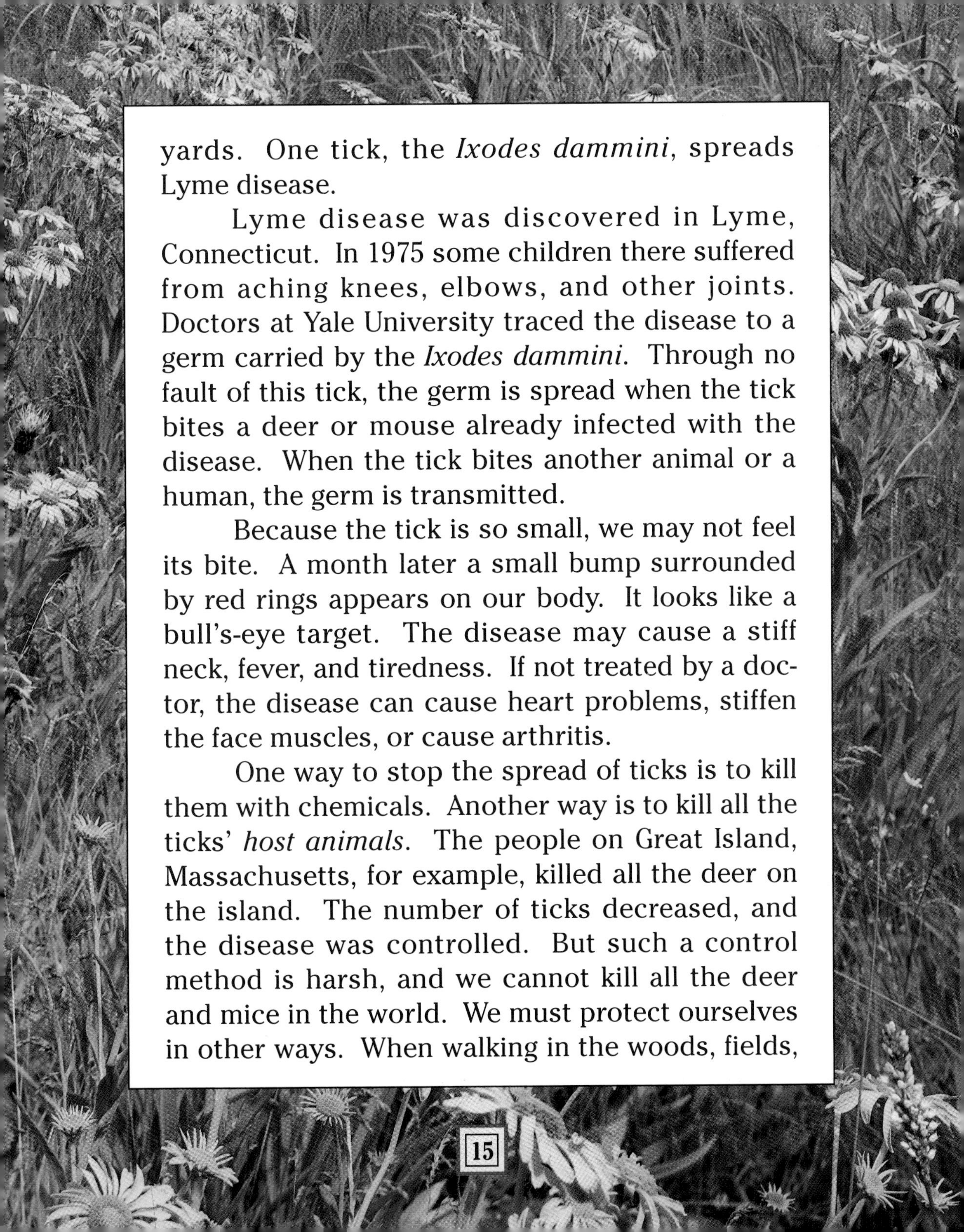

yards. One tick, the *Ixodes dammini*, spreads Lyme disease.

Lyme disease was discovered in Lyme, Connecticut. In 1975 some children there suffered from aching knees, elbows, and other joints. Doctors at Yale University traced the disease to a germ carried by the *Ixodes dammini.* Through no fault of this tick, the germ is spread when the tick bites a deer or mouse already infected with the disease. When the tick bites another animal or a human, the germ is transmitted.

Because the tick is so small, we may not feel its bite. A month later a small bump surrounded by red rings appears on our body. It looks like a bull's-eye target. The disease may cause a stiff neck, fever, and tiredness. If not treated by a doctor, the disease can cause heart problems, stiffen the face muscles, or cause arthritis.

One way to stop the spread of ticks is to kill them with chemicals. Another way is to kill all the ticks' *host animals.* The people on Great Island, Massachusetts, for example, killed all the deer on the island. The number of ticks decreased, and the disease was controlled. But such a control method is harsh, and we cannot kill all the deer and mice in the world. We must protect ourselves in other ways. When walking in the woods, fields, or tall grasses, wear light-colored clothing so the dark-colored tick can be seen on your clothes. Tuck your pants into your socks. Wear long-sleeved shirts. Always check your body for ticks after a hike. Put tick collars on your dog and cat so they cannot carry a tick inside your home.

Common Name: Grasshopper
Order: Orthoptera (straight winged)
Number of species: 20,000
Habitat: Field plants
Life span: Eggs hibernate over winter; adults four to six months
Diet: Plant leaves, stems, and juices

Grasshoppers are vegetarians. They eat leaves and stems or suck plant juices. If enough of them chew and suck on a field of corn, wheat, oats, or rye, they might destroy a farmer's entire crop.

In fact, history tells us that some have done just that. Locusts, another name for grasshoppers, were a problem for the ancient Egyptians, Greeks, and Romans. These grasshopppers grew to as much as 2 inches (5.08 cm) long. They have short, curved antennae and powerful hind legs for jumping. Some species have strong wings. A swarm of one such species in east Africa was measured at 100 feet (30.48 m) high and a mile (1.6 km) wide! Locust swarms damaged crops severly in our own plains states from 1938 to 1940. The high-plains grasshopper still damages crops in western states.

In 1848 a grasshopper called the Mormon cricket attacked the crops of Mormon settlers in Salt Lake City, Utah. This grasshopper can be brown, black, or green. It has long, thin, curved antennae and a hard shell on its back that protects the joint between its head and thorax. The Mormon cricket has no wings.

The settlers had no *insecticides* to stop the millions of crickets from invading their fields. The Mormons dug ditches around their fields and filled them with moving water to sweep the crickets away before they entered the fields. They even built short fences around the fields to stop the crickets. These methods helped, but didn't prevent all the crickets from eating the crops. The settlers thought they would starve. But, just in time, sea gulls arrived from the islands in Great Salt Lake and ate the crickets. In this case, nature solved the Mormons' problem.

These grasshoppers, and any insect that feeds on a plant so much it hurts or kills it, are called pests. An insect *pest* hurts people either by biting and carrying diseases, such as the mosquito; or like some grasshoppers, by damaging the food we eat.

Crop destruction by the Mormon cricket almost caused starvation for the settlement at Salt Lake City, Utah.

Common Name: Cicada
Order: Homoptera
(insect groups that don't
fit other categories)
Family: Cicadidae
Number of species:
1,500
Habitat: Adults, in trees; nymphs,
underground
Life span: Adults, two months; nymphs,
seventeen years
Diet: Plant juices

Another crop-destroying insect is the seventeen-year cicada. This insect lives in the ground for seventeen years as a nymph sucking on the roots of trees. As an adult, it leaves the ground and perches in branches "singing" to us from the tops of the trees. Cicadas become meals for blue jays and other birds, but enough of them survive to lay their eggs on tree twigs. These eggs hatch into nymphs. The nymphs drop to the ground, dig tunnels in the soil, and attach themselves to tree roots to begin the seventeen-year cycle.

After seventeen years feeding underground, the adult cicada emerges to lay its eggs in tree twigs.

A large *infestation* of cicadas can kill a tree either by sucking sap out of its roots or by piercing too many twigs and branches to lay their eggs.

Nature helps control destructive insects by supplying insects that eat other insects. The wasp, which we may avoid because of its painful sting, is actually one of our best friends.

CHAPTER 3
The Stingers: Wasps and Hornets

paper wasp

Order: Hymenoptera (transparent wings)
Suborder: Apocrita
Wasp family: Braconidae, Ichneumonidae, Chalcididae, Sphecidae
Hornet family: Vespidae
Number of species: 100,000
Habitat: Nests underground or on buildings
Life span: Queens, several years; hives, one summer
Diet: Young eat insects or spiders; adults eat plant juices

A wasp or hornet looks like a head and two tear drops joined together with a string. Its thorax and abdomen are pinched in the middle, making a very narrow waist. They have transparent, membrane wings with few veins. Both wasps and hornets can sting many times. Some species have long, curved antennae and some have short ones.

Solitary wasps and hornets live alone, building their nests, laying eggs, and feeding their young. Social wasps and hornets live in groups and each member does its own work in a *hive* just like that of social bees.

A digger wasp is a solitary wasp. Using her jaws and two front legs, the female takes five hours to dig a tunnel 7 inches (17.78 cm) deep. When her underground nest is finished, she hunts for long-horned grasshoppers to feed her larva. When she finds one, she stings it to paralyze the grasshopper. The wasp picks up the grasshopper in its jaws and flies back to her nest. There she places the grasshopper on its back and lays an egg on its abdomen.

The wasp egg hatches into a larva that will then eat the living grasshopper. It will take five grasshoppers to feed the larva until it is ready to spin its cocoon and *pupate* into an adult wasp. During her lifetime, the digger wasp will make six burrows or more, filling them with eggs and grasshoppers. Each digger wasp can kill as many as thirty grasshoppers during its lifetime. Ten months after the larvae spin their cocoons, they become adult wasps. They crawl to the surface and mate, and the young females dig tunnels to lay their eggs, thus renewing the cycle.

Another solitary wasp, the giant cicada killer, attacks only cicadas. This wasp may fly far from its nest, looking for cicadas to feed its larvae. Much smaller than its victim, this wasp's main problem is how to transport its heavy prey back to her nest. The giant cicada killer drags its paralyzed prey up the nearest tree. When she is about a foot up the tree, she leaps in the direction of her nest. Clutching the cicada, the wasp glides and flies until gravity pulls both to the ground. This

The giant cicada killer drags off its paralyzed prey to feed her larvae.

wasp will continue climbing and flying until it gets the cicada up to its nest.

The wasps we see most frequently are social wasps. They build paperlike nests by chewing up wood and bark strips. Hornets and yellow jackets are paper wasps. Hornets usually suspend their pear-shaped nests from trees but can also build their nests in the ground.

Social wasps hunt destructive insects but without paralyzing them or laying their eggs on them. Instead, they chew up their prey and feed the paste to their young. As the larvae are fed the insect paste, they give off drops of a sweet liquid that in turn feeds the adults. The adults feed the young and then the young feed the adults. Now that's cooperation!

There are usually two thousand wasps in a single nest. A queen wasp can lay as many as twenty-five thousand eggs in one summer! All of these thousands of larvae feed on other insects. Many of the insects they eat are harmful to our crops and gardens. But not all wasps eat all types of insects.

Certain wasps and hornets eat only certain insects. Mud daubers eat spiders. Sand wasps eat flies. The great black wasp and the golden digger wasp eat grasshoppers. Braconid wasps lay

A living but paralyzed grasshopper will feed one of the larvae of this golden digger wasp.

their eggs on sphinx moths. Some Ichneumon wasps lay eggs on sphinx moths and silk moth caterpillars that also eat tree leaves and plants. The yellow jacket feeds on crickets. There is even a wasp called the tarantula hawk that attacks the tarantula spider in the southwest. The blue mud dauber feeds her young with black widow spiders.

What is amazing about wasps and hornets is that they hunt insects only to feed their young. Most adult wasps are vegetarians that feed on nectar and sap.

Other insects live on vegetable plants and flowers. Their feeding habits can ravage an entire garden.

PART THREE: In the Garden

CHAPTER 4
The Suckers: Scales and Aphids

Order: Homoptera (insect groups that don't fit other categories)
Family: Coccoidea (scales)
Number of species: 4,000
Family: Aphididae (aphids)
Number of species: 4,000
Habitat: Trees, plants, and bushes
Life span: Eggs live through the winter; adults, one to three months
Diet: Plant juices

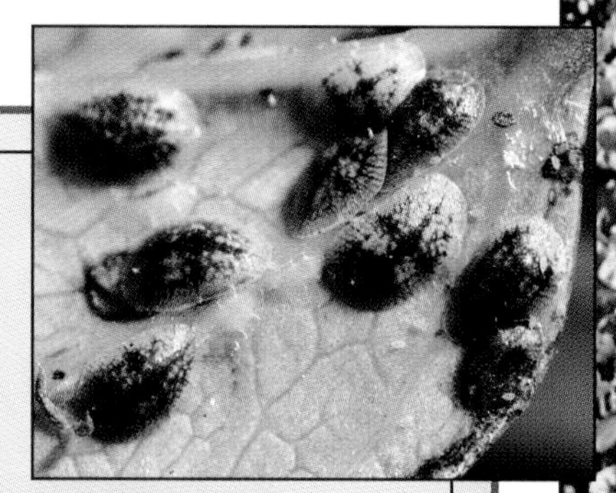

scales

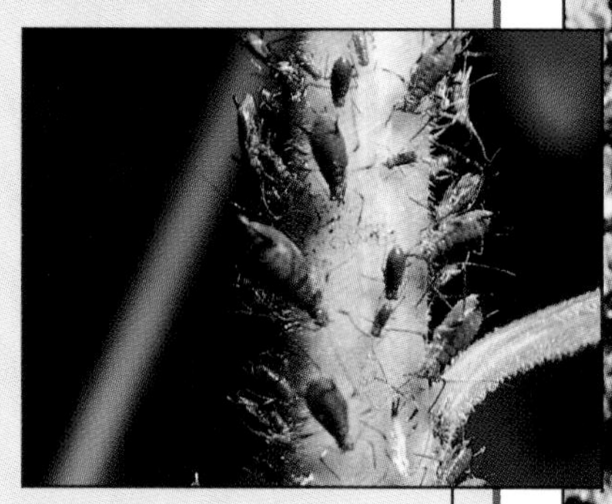

aphids with young

One large family of insects is called scales. Scales are small and round and reproduce rapidly in great numbers. Female scales stick their *proboscis* (tubelike mouths) into plants and never move from this position again. They have no wings. Male scales have no mouths and never eat. Scales cover their bodies with a waxy substance.

Many scale insects are beneficial to people. The lac scale of China, India, Burma, and Thailand produces a gummy substance called *lac*. When melted, strained, and rehardened, lac forms shellac used to make varnish and to stiffen shoes and hats. Artificial fruits and flowers, ink, dental plates, hair dyes, sealing wax, and paints all contain lac. The male Chinese wax scale makes a white wax called pe-la. Pe-la is used in candles and to stiffen paper and silk. Some Chinese believe pe-la stops bleeding, eases pain, and helps heal broken bones. The wax from a Mexican mealybug, also a scale, produces dyes still used in coloring foods, drinks, and lipsticks. The ancient Phoenicians and the Romans used another scale as a source of scarlet dye. These dyes were so precious that when the Romans took over Spain, they made that country pay them a fee, half of which was paid in scale insect dye.

Dyes produced by the Mexican mealybug are still used to color foods, drinks, and lipsticks.

Because the scale can suck a plant until it dies, they can be a pest to farmers and gardeners. The cottony-cushion scale was brought to California from Australia and almost destroyed the orange groves in that state. The San Jose scale feeds on fruit and ornamental trees. The oystershell scale feeds on walnut and other trees. The California red scale prefers orange trees.

If left alone, the aphid can produce so many young that they can devour an entire garden. Only a tenth of an inch (about .25 cm) long, the aphid females produce live young without having to mate with a male. They reproduce so rapidly that one scientist, using a strong magnifying glass, saw a baby aphid inside a bigger baby aphid inside a mother aphid. Three generations in one bug! An aphid can give birth to a dozen offspring in a day. With a strong magnifying glass, you can watch an aphid giving birth.

A mother aphid doesn't even stop eating to give birth!

Aphids can reproduce as many as thirty generations in one summer. Two American *entomologists*, W. P. Flint and C. L. Metcalf, once estimated that there were 30 million aphids on one tulip tree alone. Before computers were invented, another scientist used pencil and paper to figure that one aphid mother could produce almost 6 million offspring in one season. All those aphids laid end to end would equal 27,950 miles (about 44,980 km)—enough aphids to circle the equator with hundreds of miles left over! Fortunately, there are never that many aphids, because many are eaten by other insects, as we will see in the next chapter.

Aphids have yard ants for protectors. The aphids produce a sweet liquid called honeydew that yard ants eat. Because they function like farmers getting milk from a cow, these ants are called insect farmers. The ants, using their antennae, stroke the backends of aphids. The aphid gives them a drop of honeydew. The ants, meanwhile, chase away ladybugs, lacewing larvae, and other insects that eat aphids.

Not only do aphids injure plants by piercing them, they also transmit diseases that plague beans, sugar cane, cucumbers, and other vegetables.

In exchange for keeping away predators, this yard ant feeds on aphid honeydew.

There are other sucking bugs that can hurt plants such as squash bugs on pumpkins, the harlequin cabbage bug on cabbage and other mustard plants, and chinch bugs that attack barley, rye, wheat, corn, and sorghum.

Aphids are *specialized* in their feeding. You won't find a pea aphid on a melon or a woolly apple aphid on a handful of beans. When a plant becomes too crowded with aphids, winged aphids are born and fly to other plants.

Here's one pumpkin being eaten by squash bugs that won't make it to Halloween.

Sometimes millions of aphids migrate. Two migrations occurred in New York City in 1943. Helped along by the wind, countless millions of aphids landed in Manhattan, covering window screens, cars, and the windows of elevated trains. People walked with newspapers on their heads. No one knows why these migrations occur.

CHAPTER 5
Lacewings and Ladybugs

Order: Neuroptera (veined, or nerve-winged)
Family: Chrysopidae (lacewings)
Number of species: 4,000
Order: Coleoptera (sheath, or protective, wings)
Family: Coccinellidae (ladybugs)
Number of Species: 5,000
Habitat: Gardens, fields, and forests
Life span: Six weeks to two years
Diet: Aphids, mealybugs, Japanese beetles

lacewing larvae

ladybug larvae

The green lacewing fly is about a half inch (1.27 cm) long and is colored pale green. It has delicate, transparent wings with veins that look like lace. It is the green lacewing larvae that help gardeners control aphids.

Green lacewing eggs hatch into larvae that eat so many aphids, they are called aphis lions. The lacewing larvae spend twelve days feasting on aphids. Small, brown, and looking like hairless spindle-shaped caterpillars, these larvae can catch, pierce, and suck out an aphid in one minute. By the end of their twelve days as larvae, these aphis lions eat almost sixty aphids per hour. Even then they are still hungry!

One type of aphis lion covers its body with the skins of the aphids it eats. It looks like a walking trash heap, but the dead skins keep it safe from other predator insects such as ants. Some aphis lions produce a smelly fluid that sticks to your hands and can smell for hours. Aphis lion adults are called the skunks of the insect world, and their strong odor keeps enemies away. None of them bite. They flutter with their green, graceful wings and are attracted to light, easy to follow, and fun to watch.

The ladybug beetle is even more useful to the gardener. Ladybugs are bright red, usually with spots on their backs. Some have two spots, some ten, some twelve, and some have no spots at all. Ladybug larvae are also spindle-shaped and wrinkled, and have short antennae. Both larvae and adult ladybugs feed on aphids and scales. The ladybug larvae are called aphis wolves. In one hour a ladybug larva can eat forty aphids.

These swarms of ladybugs protect the plant from aphids.

They eat so many of these harmful insects that a dozen ladybugs can devour all of the scales and aphids on one fruit tree.

Ladybugs saved the orange groves of California from the cottony-cushion scale. These scales, mentioned in Chapter Four, arrived in this country in 1888 in crates of Australian oranges. The scale destroyed many orange trees. To stop the destruction, the entomologist Albert Koebele

A mere dozen ladybugs like this one can protect an entire fruit tree from aphids and scales.

went to Australia and brought back the Australian ladybug. He put these ladybugs on an orange tree and covered the tree with a net. The next spring, the net was opened to let the ladybugs fly to other trees infected with the scales. All the scales on the first tree were eaten by the Australian ladybugs. Other citrus growers brought branches covered with scales from their trees. In two hours ladybugs swarmed over the branches. The growers took the ladybugs back to their own orchards. Within two years, the cottony-cushion scale was gone. The citrus groves were saved.

Ladybugs are important to potato farmers. The ladybug larvae eat the eggs of the Colorado potato beetle that feeds on potato crops. Gardeners like ladybugs, because they eat the aphids that feed on vegetable plants and rosebushes.

The bright red color of the ladybug is a warning to other insects that they taste bad. The ladybug also produces a foul-smelling fluid that keeps enemies at bay. This way, the ladybugs are left alone to fly from bush to bush, eating aphids and scales and helping gardeners.

CHAPTER 6
The Sweeties: Bees

carpenter bee

Order: Hymenoptera (transparent membrane wings)
Family: Apoidea
Number of species: 20,000
Habitat: Hives or nests, above or below ground
Life span: Queen, two to five years; workers, four to six weeks
Diet: Nectar, sap, pollen, fruit juices

Nature's best friend, and ours, is the bee. When they fly from flower to flower, sucking nectar and collecting pollen, bees play an important role in the growth of fruits and vegetables. Bees evolved from wasps a hundred million years ago.

Bumblebees, small furry insects with orange, black, and yellow bodies, live in the ground in small nests. With a tubelike proboscis and feathery hairs on its legs, the bumblebee collects nectar and pollen to feed the hive.

A bee collects pollen in special baskets near the top of its rear legs. Pollen grains from these baskets drop on the seed-producing parts of flowers. This is called *pollination*, a process necessary for plants to grow fruit. For the wild birds around a pond, it means there will be berries to eat in the fall. Pollinated cranberry plants provide sweet berries in the spring, on which birds feed when they return from the south.

Honeybees are social bees. A hive usually contains one queen, about one hundred male bees called drones, and fifty thousand or more female workers. A honeybee egg, laid by the queen, hatches into a larva within three to four days. Workers feed the larva up to 1,300 times a day by dropping into the honeycomb cell royal jelly produced by the worker bees, then nectar and pollen collected by other worker bees. After about five days, the larva is fully grown and sealed in its cell to pupate.

A worker bee performs different jobs during its lifetime. At first a worker cleans out the honeycomb's old cells. Then it feeds the newly hatched eggs or the queen. When the worker bee's wax glands develop, it builds cells in the *honeycomb*. Workers guard the entrance to the hive or take nectar from other worker bees. Finally, after about four weeks, the worker leaves the hive to find nectar and pollen. A honeybee worker lives five to six weeks while the queen lives two to five years and lays 400,000 eggs!

The end product of all this work is honey. The nectar that honeybees eat is digested into simple sugars. As the water *evaporates* from the sugar liquid, it thickens and becomes honey. The bees store the honey as food for the winter. Beekeepers take the honey from the hives for people to eat but leave enough food for the bees.

People have benefited from bees for centuries. The early peoples from Asia took honeybees with them wherever they settled. The bees were used for their honey and to pollinate crops. The ancient Egyptians, as well as the Greeks, Romans, and Europeans in the Middle Ages, also kept bees. Honeybees were brought to America in 1670 and spread westward before the wagon trains did.

Today, Americans eat 275 million pounds of honey each year. We use the beeswax from the honeycombs as a sealer and as an ingredient in

The worker bees in this hive feed their queen and care for the larva.

This busy digger bee is preparing her nest in the ground.

polishes and floor waxes. It can take the bees 37,000 trips to collect enough nectar to make one pound of honey. That could mean 50,000 miles (80,465 km) of bee flights visiting 2 million different flowers! Different kinds of honey are named for the flowers that bees visit: clover honey, buckwheat honey, orange blossom, and goldenrod honey.

The honeybees' most important job is pollination. Farmers and gardeners depend on bees to help them grow peaches, apples, alfalfa, clover, berry bushes, and vegetable plants. Beekeepers rent their hives to farmers who need fruit orchards pollinated. It would be impossible to grow some crops without bees.

Not all bees live in hives. Just as there are solitary wasps, there are solitary bees. Digger bees dig 2-inch (5.08 cm) tunnels in the ground. Mason bees use sand, dirt, and saliva to build nests in the cracks and walls of buildings. Leaf-cutting bees live in the ground or in hollow logs and cut circles of leaves to use in their nests. They particularly like rosebush leaves. Carpenter bees thrive in wood.

Most insects live outdoors in a world of their own. Some, however, have moved into our homes.

PART FOUR: In the House

CHAPTER 7
Cockroaches, Flies, and Other House Dwellers

Common Name: Cockroaches
Order: Orthoptera (straight winged)
Family: Blattidae (cockroaches)
Number of species: 2,250
Habitat: Jungles, forests, house holds
Life span: Five months to two years
Diet: Rotted meat, vegetation, wood, leaves, paper

Cockroaches have survived on Earth for 300 million years. Scientists think they developed wings before birds did. Roaches have flattened, brown bodies. They live everywhere except in the coldest areas. They scurry to slip into cracks and crevices. They almost always scurry away before we catch them.

Cockroaches are night scavengers. And they eat almost anything. Only a few types of cockroaches live with people. The most common is the ½-inch-long (1.27-cm) German roach. Most roaches live in forests where their scavenging habits help clean up the woods and keep them healthy. Roaches are an important part of the food chain.

In our homes, cockroaches can live in bookcases and bathrooms, kitchens and cabinets. It's almost impossible to starve a cockroach. In every place it lives, it can find something to eat. The best way to control their numbers is to keep our homes clean. Place all garbage in tightly closed containers and do not leave any foods on the tables or counters uncovered.

Other insects that live in our households are mostly little creatures that dash out of corners and surprise us in basements. Most household insects do not harm people.

Silverfish, an insect with a body that looks like the top of an exclamation point, live around kitchen and bathroom pipes and on basement floors. Silverfish eat wallpaper paste, the glue on book covers, and even paper.

Earwigs use the tweezerlike pincers on their abdomen to defend themselves. The pinch is not dangerous, but you'll feel it! Earwigs feed on dead insects, rotting grass or plants, and scraps of food on the floor. They got their name because people mistakenly thought that they crawled into people's ears while they slept.

The silverfish scurries around kitchen and bathroom pipes and in our basements.

The earwig got its name from a legend that said the insect liked to crawl in people's ears.

Clothes moths lay eggs in coats and suits. Their larvae chew bits and pieces of fabric to make a nest, leaving holes behind. "Don't let the bed bugs bite" is a saying that started years ago when the bed bug, another household insect, was common in homes. Because we have cleaner habits, bed bugs are not the problem they used to be.

Common Name: Fleas
Order: Siphonaptera
(suckers, no wings)
Number of species: 1,000
Habitat: Forests, fields, households
Life span: Over a year
Diet: Blood

The flea is a household insect that can pose a health threat to humans. All fleas suck blood from animals.

The common dog flea is not dangerous. But the fleas that live on mice and rats can spread a disease call *bubonic plague*. Bubonic plague has killed millions of people through the centuries. Historians estimate that 25 million people lost their lives in Europe in 1348 because of the plague. During the Great Plague of London in 1665, 60,000 to 100,000 people died. In the late 1800s, 3 million people in India succumbed to the plague in a span of ten years. There are still outbreaks of plague in the world today in Namibia and Angola. Because scientists found the antibiotics tetracycline and streptomycin to treat it, plague is no longer a devastating threat.

Common Name: Flies
Order: Diptera (two-winged animals)
Number of species: 40,000
Habitat: Barns, stables, households
Life span: Adults hibernate over winter
Diet: Manure and table food

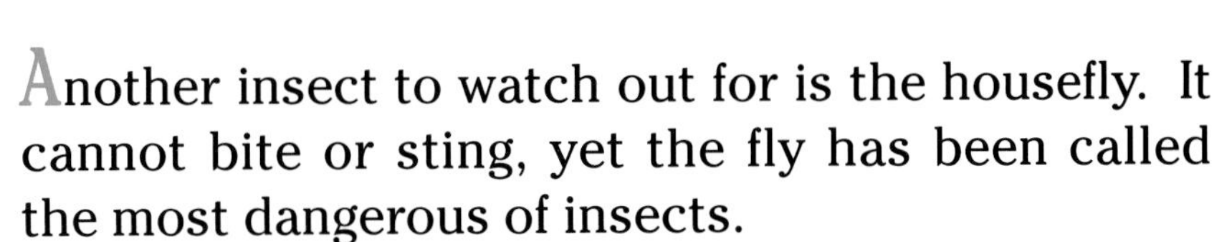

Another insect to watch out for is the housefly. It cannot bite or sting, yet the fly has been called the most dangerous of insects.

Flies thrive wherever there is pollution and decay. Flies lay their eggs on animal manure, dead animals, in stables, outhouses, and garbage pails. In this filth live millions of *bacteria* and *protozoa*. These germs get caught on the hairs of the fly's body and the sticky pads on its feet. One scientist counted over 6 million germs on a single fly.

When a housefly feeds on our food, its proboscis injects the food with saliva to make it liquid. As it sucks up the now-liquid food, it leaves behind small specks of its own manure. Then it flies away. Each time a fly walks, using the sticky pads on its feet, it leaves behind some of the germs stuck there when it last visited a pile of manure or garbage.

If they carry the germ, flies can spread *typhoid fever*. During the Spanish-American War in 1898, flies carrying the typhoid germ killed five thousand soldiers. Ironically, only four thousand soldiers died in battle. Typhoid fever and other diseases carried by flies are not the problem today that they were in the past. As more people moved away from farms and stables, as they built sewers to carry away their own wastes, and as people kept cleaner homes and farms, the number of places where flies could breed and pick up harmful germs decreased. Today's flies do not come into contact with the numbers of germs they used to, so they usually cannot infect us.

Insects that inhabit our households are mostly annoying and sometimes dangerous. But, even in our households, nature helps control indoor insects with the spiders—a formidable predator of many insects.

CHAPTER 8

The Swingers: House Spiders

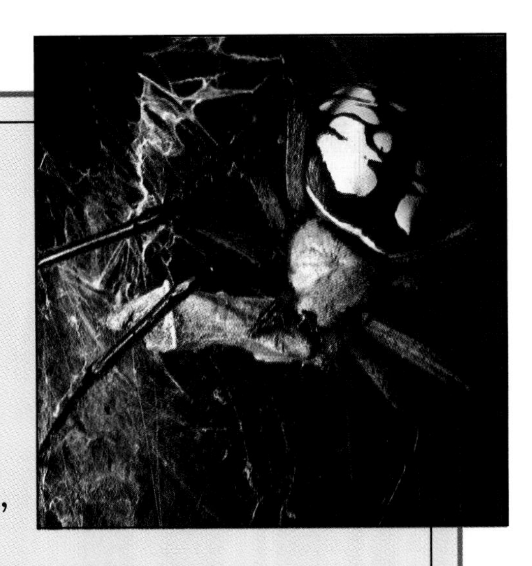

Class: Arachnida (eight-legged animals)
Number of species: 30,000
Habitat: On land anywhere from marshes to deserts, households, barns
Life span: One to seven years
Diet: Insects

The best natural control of flies is the spider. Spiders are not insects. All insects have six legs. Spiders, like ticks, have eight.

House spiders are true helpmates if we leave them alone. Like the garden spider, the house spider builds a web. Not as pretty as the outdoor webs, this one looks like a three-sided trampoline with a sag in the middle. House spiders build their nests in the high corners of rooms, cellars, and attics. While the house spider hides in a tube built near the botton of the web, a fly is trapped in the web. Quickly the spider pulls the fly into the tube and eats its prey in peace, out of sight.

Most spiders live only one year and die when the weather turns cold. House spiders live five to seven years in our warm homes. Spiders eat all insects, even those that benefit people. One scientist estimated that the thirty thousand types of spiders everywhere eat so many insects in a single day that the total outweighs all the people on Earth! Outdoors, spiders pick from a menu ranging from aphids on pecan trees, to moths that lay eggs that grow into worms in apples, to the spruce budworm that attacks spruce and fir trees.

Indoors, spiders eat flies, cockroaches, and earwigs. Unfortunately, most people do not want spiders in their homes any more than they want flies. The webs attract dirt and dust along with insects.

Some people fear a spider's bite. Most spiders cannot bite through our thick skin. Even though their bite is poisonous to the insects they trap, it is not so to humans. Spiders such as the tarantula and the black widow, however, can bite through our skin. These spiders are actually shy, but because they live near people, they are found in surprising places—sometimes inside people's shoes. If they feel threatened, they will bite.

Bites from the tarantula spider are no longer deadly to humans thanks to medicine developed by scientists.

Although it's painful, scientists now know their bite is usually harmless to humans. Doctors developed an antivenin, *Lactrodectus mactans* to cure people with strong reactions to the black widow bite.

In warmer climates where there are many more insects, people truly want spiders in their homes. In some villages in Mexico, swarms of flies invade homes during the rainy season. To combat the flies, the villagers collect webs from a spider called the mosquero. They place these webs in their homes and the spiders catch the flies.

Spiders and their webs are useful for reasons other than trapping insects. The aborigines of Northern Queensland use spider webs and sticks for fishing poles. Manufacturers are trying to make clothing out of spider silk. Scientists are studying the use of spider venom to treat brain damage among people who have strokes, Alzheimer's disease, and other brain disorders. Other scientists hope to use spider silk to make artificial heart valves and veins. Spider silk may someday be used in bulletproof vests to make them lighter.

As we learn more and more about insects, we can appreciate their importance in food chains

Perhaps if our indoor spiders spun webs as pretty as this we wouldn't mind them hanging in our corners!

all over the world. If all the insects suddenly died, many animals that depend on them for food would also die. Some of our fruits, vegetables, and flowers would cease to exist. To help control disease, grow our crops, and even to provide us with carbon, nature's basic building block, insects are essential to our lives.

GLOSSARY

Abdomen—the third and usually the largest of the three sections of an insect's body.

Antennae—two jointed and flexible organs on an insect's head, used to sense food, heat, and danger. Antennae can be long, short, curved, straight, or bent.

Arachnids—eight-legged animals, such as spiders and ticks, that belong to the class Arachnida.

Arthritis—a disease that causes swelling and pain in body joints such as the knees, fingers, hips, etc.

Bacteria—one-celled organisms. Some are beneficial, particularly those that help turn rotting vegetation into carbon. Others are harmful because they produce disease.

Bubonic plague—popularly known as the Black Plague, this disease causes fevers, vomiting, and painful sores on the skin.

Carbon—a nonmetallic element found in all living things; the basic element for life.

Egg rafts—groups of eggs, sometimes as many as four hundred, laid on top of still patches of water by adult female mosquitoes.

Element—a single substance that cannot be broken down into smaller parts.

Entomologist—a scientist who studies insects.

Evaporate— to remove water from something and make it thicker.

Evolved—slowly changed body parts, feeding habits, or favorite places to live that usually takes centuries.

Food chain—a natural cummunity, such as the woods, where plants and animals use each other as food.

Hive—the home, made of cells, for social bees and wasps. Most often used as the name for the honeybees' home and started by the queen, the hive is built by the worker bees to store honey and raise more bees.

Honeycomb—the grouping of six-sided wax cells within a hive built by honeybees to hold eggs and store honey.

Host animal—an animal that another animal lives on or in.

Infestation—so many insects gathering in a single area that they become harmful to the plant life there.

Lac—a thick, clear substance produced by the lac scale. It is used in shellac (to treat wood). It is also used in paints, records, and dental plates, and to add stiffness to hats and shoes.

Larva—an insect that has hatched from an egg. Often it looks very different from the adult.

Metamorphosis—the stages an insect passes through to become an adult. Complete metamorphosis is made up of four stages: egg, larva, pupa, and adult; incomplete, or simple, metamorphosis has three stages: egg, nymph, and adult.

Nymph—the young of any insect that has incomplete, or simple, metamorphosis.

Paralyze—to make an insect unable to move.

Pest—an insect that hurts humans either by spreading diseases or by damaging food crops.

Pollination—the process of fertilizing a plant by placing pollen on the female part of the flower.

Proboscis—a long, tubelike mouth for sucking; like a vaccination needle, only much smaller.

Protozoa—a group of organisms that are single-celled and include the simplest animals known to us such as the amoeba.

Pupate—to be inactive in a cocoon; to undergo the third stage in complete metamorphosis.

Saliva—watery, tasteless liquid in the mouth that helps digest food.

Specialized—needing a certain food or place to live.

Species—a type of animal or plant that can mate only with others like itself.

Swarm—a large group of insects such as honeybees and their queen or grasshoppers and crickets that moves together, searching for a new home or feeding areas.

Thorax—the middle section of the three connecting parts of an insect's body.

Transmit—to cause the spread of a disease.

Typhoid fever—a disease spread by flies that caused many deaths in the past but is now controlled by cleanliness.

Yellow fever—a disease spread by mosquitoes which causes fever, headache, and vomiting. After three days the fever drops, and the skin that a lemon-yellow color from which the disease gets its name.

FOR FURTHER READING

Blassingame, Wyatt. *The Little Killers: Fleas, Lice, Mosquitos.* New York: G. P. Putnam's Sons, 1975.

Cole, Joanna. *Cockroaches.* New York: William Morrow & Co., 1971.

Edsall, Marian S. *Battle on the Rosebush. Insect Life in Your Backyard.* Chicago: Follett Publishing Co., 1972.

Hoke, Helen, and Valerie Pitt. *Fleas.* New York: Franklin Watts, Inc., 1974.

Hutchins, Ross E. *The Bug Clan.* New York: Dodd, Mead & Co. 1973.

Hutchins, Ross E. *The Cicada.* Addison-Wesley, 1971.

Hutchins, Ross E. *Grasshoppers and Their Kin.* New York: Dodd, Mead & Co., 1972.

McClung, Robert M. *Bees, Wasps, and Hornets and How They Live.* New York: William Morrow & Co., 1971.

McClung, Robert M. *Ladybug.* New York: William Morrow & Co., 1966.

Stidworthy, John. *Insects.* New York: Gloucester Press, 1989.

Webster, David. *Let's Find Out About Mosquitos.* New York: Franklin Watts, Inc., 1974.

INDEX

Acarina, 14
Africa, 17
Alzheimer's disease, 54
Angola, 48
Antibiotics, 49
Ants, 30
Aphididae, 26
Aphids, 26, 29-32, 37
    Pea, 31
    Woolly apple, 31
Apocrita, 21
Apoidea, 38
Arachnida, 14, 51
Arachnids, 14
Arthropoda, 6, 7
Asia, 40
Australia, 28, 37, 54
Bed bugs, 47
Bees, 13, 38
    Bumblebees, 38
    Carpenter, 43
    Digger, 43
    Honeybees, 39
    Leaf-cutting, 43
    Mason, 43
    Social, 39
    Solitary, 43
Birds, 8
Blattidae, 44
Blue jays, 19
Bubonic plague, 48
Burma, 27
Butterflies, 13
California, 28
Carbon, 7, 8
China, 27
Chinch bugs, 31
Cicadas, 23, 24
Coccoidea, 26
Cockroaches, 13, 44-45, 52
    German, 45
Colorado potato beetle, 37
Crickets, 25
Deer, 15
Diptera, 49
Dragonflies, 12
Earwigs, 46, 52
Egg rafts, 11
Egyptians, 17, 40
Exoskeletons, 7
Fish, 8
Fleas, 48-49
Flies, 13, 44, 49-50, 52
Flint, W.P., 30

Food chain, 7, 11, 13, 55
Frogs, 8
Giant water bug, 8
Grasshoppers, 16, 18, 22, 24
    Mormon crickets, 17-18
Great Island
  (Massachusetts), 15
Great Plague of London, 48
Great Salt Lake, 18
Greeks, 17, 40
Harlequin cabbage bugs, 31
Hexapoda, 6, 7
Hive, 22, 40
Homoptera, 19, 26
Honeydew, 30
Hornets, 21, 22, 24
    Social, 22
    Solitary, 22
Host animals, 15
Hymenoptera, 21, 38
India, 27
Insecticides, 17
Insects, 6-7
Lac, 27
Lacewings, 30, 34
Ladybugs, 30
    Australian, 37
Locusts, 17
Lyme (Connecticut), 15
Lyme disease, 15
Manhattan, 32
Metamorphosis, 7
Metcalf, C.L., 30
Mexico, 54
Mice, 15
Mormon crickets, 17-18
Mormons, 17-18
Mosquitoes, 11-12, 18
Moths, 13, 47
Mud daubers, 24
Namibia, 48
New York City (New York),
  32
Orthoptera, 16, 44
Pe-la, 27
Pests, 18
Phoenicians, 27
Pollen, 39
Romans, 17, 27, 40
Salt Lake City (Utah), 17
Scales, 26-28, 37
    California red, 28
    Chinese wax, 27
    Lac, 27

Mexican mealybug, 27
Oystershell, 28
San Jose, 28
Shellac, 27
Silk moths, 25
Silverfish, 46
Siphonaptera, 48
Snails, 8
Snakes, 8
Spanish-American War, 11, 50
Sphinx moths, 25
Spiders, 24, 51-54
Black widow, 25, 53-54
Garden, 51
House, 51, 52
Mosquero, 54
Tarantula, 25, 53
Squash bugs, 31
Tadpoles, 8
Tarantulas, 25
Thailand, 27
Ticks, 14-16, 51
Ixodes dammini, 15
Typhoid fever, 50
Vespidae, 21
Vietnam War, 11
Wasps, 13, 22, 24, 38
Blue mud dauber, 25
Braconid, 24
Digger, 22
Giant cicada killers, 23, 24
Golden digger, 24
Great black, 24
Ichneumon, 25
Paper, 24
Sand, 24
Social, 22, 24
Solitary, 22
Tarantula hawk, 25
Water strider, 8
Yale University, 15
Yellow jackets, 24, 25
Yellow fever, 11

ABOUT THE AUTHOR

Liz Greenbacker has published hundreds of articles and several books for children and adults. Before becoming a writer she spent more than twenty years as a bookkeeper, and was elected to the Meriden, CT, City Council. She has taught creative writing classes for several years, and is a staff instructor at an annual summer writing conference of the International Women's Writing Guild.

Ms. Greenbacker says that she hopes *Bugs* "goes beyond identifying, classifying, and describing insects. This book shows how [bugs] fit into the grand scheme of our planet, how they can hurt us and how many of them help us." To help keep motivated while writing this book, she kept a rubber spider attached to the top of her compter with its legs dangling in front of the screen.